BREEDERS' BEST
A KENNEL CLUB BOOK™

# German Shepherd Dog

By Meg Purnell-Carpenter

# BREEDERS' BEST
### A KENNEL CLUB BOOK™

# GERMAN SHEPHERD DOG

ISBN: 1-59378-903-3

**Copyright © 2004**

Kennel Club Books, LLC
308 Main Street, Allenhurst, NJ 07711 USA
Printed in South Korea

*PHOTOS BY:*
Isabelle Français
and Bernd Brinkmann.

*DRAWINGS BY:*
Yolyanko el Habanero.

# Contents

# Meet the German Shepherd Dog

L ong before the dawn of modern times, man shared his hearth with dog-like creatures. Primitive drawings from the Stone Age era and ancient archaeological finds trace the development of the domesticated dog and the establishment of distinct breeds from antiquity to modern times.

Much of that history describes wolf-like dogs with outstanding herding instincts that guarded their charges with unswerving loyalty and

Originally developed and bred by a German cavalry officer, the GSD excels in military work. First employed by German forces, the GSD has become the dog of choice for troops around the world, including those of the US.

courage. During early European civilization, such dogs were bred for their useful qualities, with no thought or concern for conformation or consistent physical properties other than utilitarian. Instinct, intelligence and courage were primary, and shepherds chose only the best canine specimens from which to breed their working stock. The size of the dog's ears or the angulation of its hocks didn't matter—only how well the dog could herd sheep!

Wolves and dogs belong to the same genus and are closely related, with the earliest domesticated dogs counting the wolf as their direct ancestor.

In Germany, as in other European countries, specific types of shepherding dogs evolved. In 1899 a German cavalry officer, Max von Stephanitz, took notice of a hard-working shepherd dog and launched a program to standardize and promote the breed. Von Stephanitz purchased Hektor von Linkshein, whom he thought to be an outstanding example of true herding type. Renamed Horand von Grafrath,

The German Shepherd Dog today still possesses the same wonderful qualities of loyalty, work ethic and intelligence like no other in dogdom. Nico is a handsome five-year-old from the breed's homeland.

this dog became the foundation upon which all German Shepherd Dogs would follow.

Von Stephanitz's dedication to the breed is legendary. He founded the *Verein für Deutsche Schäferhunde* (SV), the German breed club, which became the largest specialty club in the world, with 1,600 local clubs and almost 80,000 members. Through the SV, von Stephanitz exerted tremendous influence over German breeding programs. He was also the impetus behind the Shepherd's adaptation as German law-enforcement and military dogs and eventually as guide dogs for the blind.

The German Shepherd's rapid rise to fame and popularity is a tribute to both dog and man. Von Stephanitz campaigned to preserve the German Shepherd as a courageous working family companion, and his efforts helped to gain the public's notice of the breed. Shepherds competed in both dog shows and working/herding trials, and the dog's natural beauty, character and noble bearing quickly captured the heart of the dog-owning world. Breed popularity spread across the Atlantic; in 1911, the German Shepherd Dog was recognized by the American Kennel Club (AKC).

During World War I, the GSD gained fame as a messenger and sentry dog for both sides of the conflict. Stories of the breed's heroic feats during battle spread throughout Europe and the United States. Eventually, images of the famous Rin-Tin-Tin flashed across movie screens and later graced home television sets.

German Shepherds served America again in World War II and have performed nobly in many subsequent US military conflicts. The most widely used breed in the military, they are considered working soldiers who are highly valuable to America's defense system. Trained to patrol, control crowds and detect narcotics and explosives, they also support the Secret Service in protecting the president and other important political dignitaries. Most serve for about ten years, and retired dogs are available for adoption by both members of the military and civilians.

It was not surprising when this consummate working dog began multi-tasking as a police dog and search-and-rescue dog, and later as guide dog, assistance dog, hearing dog, drug and bomb detector, sentry and service dog. The German Shepherd Dog soon sky-rocketed to one of the ten most popular AKC-registered breeds.

Sadly, breed quality soon suffered a decline as for-profit breeders capitalized on the breed's popularity and produced atypical GSDs with poor temperaments, unsound structures and many health problems. However, during the past several decades responsible breeders have worked hard to restore and preserve the true heart, health and physical soundness of the working Shepherd. Today you can find stable, healthy

Without hesitation, the German Shepherd nimbly navigates the rubble of a collapsed building, using his skills and instincts to locate survivors. Heartwarming stories abound of the breed's heroics.

German Shepherd Dogs if you search out reputable breeders who are dedicated to their beloved breed.

The ideal German Shepherd is an excellent family companion, a highly intelligent dog who is easily trained if handled with positive reinforcement and firm, gentle consistency. He is good with children if well supervised and is good with other pets if he is socialized with them at an early age. He is active and job-oriented and is best raised in an environment that offers ample opportunity for work and exercise.

The Shepherd is a loyal and courageous fellow who is intuitive of his owner's needs and emotions. He is reserved

It is sometimes necessary for a rescue-dog-and-handler team to be lowered into otherwise inaccessible areas to do their work. The GSD's participation in such daring rescue missions speaks volumes about the breed's remarkable courage and ability to trust humans.

and aloof with strangers and is an excellent watchdog. His size and authoritative demeanor can be intimidating and are excellent deterrents to those who might threaten or harm his human family.

German Shepherds carry medium-length, thick double coats that shed profusely twice a year, so frequent to daily brushing is required for a healthy coat and a livable household. The average lifespan is 12 to 14 years, but the breed is plagued with multiple health problems, which can affect the length and quality of the GSD's life. Buying your puppy from a qualified responsible breeder is the first step you can take to making sure that your Shepherd has a fair shake at his true lifespan.

Despite the German Shepherd Dog's sterling qualities, it is not a breed for everyone. This dog needs a job, and he requires an owner who is equal to the dog's intelligence and is committed to a full-time partnership with his dog.

## MEET THE GERMAN SHEPHERD DOG

### Overview

- Max von Stephanitz, a German cavalry officer, regulated breeding programs, founded the German breed club and was responsible for the breed's introduction to military, police and guide-dog work.
- The German Shepherd Dog was recognized in the US in 1911 and became an indispensable helper to the American military, continuing to present times.
- The GSD's popularity has led to indiscriminate breeding, but true breeders work to protect the breed's health and good reputation.

# Description of the GSD

No breed of dog is more impressive than the German Shepherd Dog. His handsome appearance and noble bearing are those of a true aristocrat, a dog whose strength and intelligence are apparent even to the most casual observer. As one of the youngest of the world's recognized dog breeds, the German Shepherd's rapid rise to fame is ample evidence of his magnetic and widespread appeal.

Although the first serious attempt to standardize the German Shepherd Dog occurred in the late 1800s,

The impressive head, striking coloration and alert expression combine to create a dog that embodies dignity and intelligence.

canine shepherds have worked with human shepherds for many centuries, herding and guarding sheep, cattle and other animals. Dogs of old were prized for their herding ability, intelligence, courage and dedication to the flock, and herdsmen bred their dogs to preserve and enhance those qualities.

Perhaps the most overlooked skill of the German Shepherd Dog is right there in the breed's name! The GSD has been used for such a multitude of tasks that he is rarely thought of first as a herding breed.

When German cavalryman and breeder Max von Stephanitz founded the German club for German Shepherds in 1899, he sought to ensure that working ability would remain as important as physical appearance. Von Stephanitz had much influence in regulating German breeding programs, and those years of calculated breeding have imprinted the GSD with signature qualities that set the breed apart from other multi-purpose canines.

When you think of a guide dog, you think of the German Shepherd. This breed is implicitly trusted by its sight-impaired owners to lead the way and protect them from danger.

All pure-bred dogs are bred according to a breed standard, the official description of the ideal for that breed, detailing correct structure, temperament, movement and performance characteristics. Written by the breed's parent club and approved by the American Kennel Club (AKC), this blueprint serves as a guideline for judging dogs in conformation. Other registries throughout the world set forth their own breed standards as well. Without such a canine formula, all the qualities so valued in the German Shepherd could be diluted or lost completely over time.

The AKC and the *Verein für Deutsche Schäferhunde* (SV), the official club for German Shepherd Dogs in Germany, have similar breed standards, with the German standard more rigid and explicit. To protect the true characteristics of the breed, the SV has established breed

The German Shepherd presents a unique profile. The overall impression of the dog's body is one of agility, power and strength.

wardens who inspect prospective breeding stock for proper structure and temperament and rate them accordingly. Breeding animals must possess a minimum of a SchH I (Schutzhund, level 1) or HGH (herding degree) before they are bred. The SV also advises breeders on other breeding issues and supervises the raising of litters.

No such restrictions govern breeders in the United States. AKC registration of the sire and dam is the only requirement to declare and register a puppy as a German Shepherd Dog.

The AKC standard describes the German Shepherd as a "strong and well muscled animal, alert and full of life." The standard further states what might be called the hallmark of the breed: "The ideal dog is stamped with a look of quality and nobility—difficult to define, but unmistakable when present." Anyone familiar with the breed understands that distinctive look.

The AKC GSD standard refers to working ability in the section on temperament, stating the dog must be "fit and willing to serve in its capacity as a companion, watchdog, blind leader, herding dog, or guardian, whichever the circumstances command." German Shepherd temperament has "a distinct personality marked by direct and fearless, but not hostile, expression, self confidence and a certain aloofness that does not extend itself to immediate and indiscriminate friendships."

The temperament section also states the dog must not be timid, nervous, anxious or lacking confidence, and that such faults are to be severely penalized. The breed's work ethic and regal personality are addressed once more in the conclusion. "The ideal dog is a working animal with an incorruptible character combined with body and gait suitable for the arduous work which constitutes its primary purpose."

The Shepherd's finely chiseled head is considered by many to be the breed's most distinctive feature. His erect, pointed ears seem to reflect his undivided attention, and his dark eyes wear an expression that is "keen, intelligent and composed" and should mirror the confidence within.

German Shepherd structure is one of grace and

Although the white German Shepherd is a nice-looking dog, this coloration is not typical in the breed and thus unacceptable according to breed standards.

Whether working in inclement weather or just enjoying a day at the beach, the German Shepherd is protected and insulated by his thick double coat.

power. The back is straight and strong, with a topline that slopes smoothly, as in the familiar Shepherd posture seen at dog shows.

In motion, the German Shepherd Dog is "a trotting dog, and its structure has been developed to meet the requirements of its work." Shepherds should gait smoothly and without effort, covering the ground with a balanced and effortless stride. One can almost envision the livestock running ahead of the Shepherd as he gears up into a flying trot.

The GSD's thick double coat insulates the dog from heat and cold, enabling him to work in the most inclement weather. Coat color varies from black and tan to sable and gray sable. White coats and non-black noses are disqualifications.

All of the elements of the breed standard are designed to preserve the true working character of the German Shepherd Dog. Although most

The gait of the athletic German Shepherd is likened to a "flying trot." The dog must be capable of covering ample ground effortlessly, whether chasing after stubborn livestock or just enjoying a jog.

modern Shepherds do not work as did their ancestors, they should still possess the ability and true spirit that distinguishes this versatile and remarkable breed.

## DESCRIPTION OF THE GSD

### Overview

- The German breed standard is very detailed; in addition, dogs are inspected and rated to determine whether they are of sufficient breeding quality.
- While not as rigid as the German standard, the AKC standard aptly outlines proper working ability and temperament along with a point-by-point description of the correct physical features as well as breed faults.
- The head is a distinct feature, imparting the breed's regal bearing and intelligence through its chiseled lines and keen expression.
- Correct gait reflects correct structure, and proper movement is so essential in a working breed that must cover much ground in order to do his job.

# Are You a GSD Person?

C an you think of a breed more noble or courageous than the German Shepherd? Today's Shepherd remains a confident and fearless protector, loyal, devoted and willing to protect at any cost.

Since the breed's rise to prominence in the 1900s, the Shepherd has excelled in every area available to canine service. Protection dog, law-enforcement partner, drug and bomb detector, search-and-rescue hero, guide and assistance dog, hearing dog...there is no breed better suited to working day after day, under extreme conditions and

The ideal GSD owner is an active person with many interests, someone who enjoys having a dog that can join her on most any of her pursuits (and hopefully knows how to put on the brakes!).

with more heart. No breed has sacrificed its life for its human partners more often.

However, such versatility does not necessarily make the GSD the best choice for the average family. Despite all of the sterling qualities that make the Shepherd a brilliant service animal, prospective owners must be aware that this is an extremely intelligent dog who takes his work very seriously. He is family-oriented and needs to be a part of his human family in both spirit and activity. He cannot be relegated to the back yard and left to his own devices. Given plenty of exercise and mega-doses of human contact, he will thrive. If neglected or unexercised, he will be bored and destructive. This is not a happy prospect with a breed as powerful as the German Shepherd.

The Shepherd's unswerving devotion to his master does not mean that he automatically understands

The German Shepherd Dog is a loyal friend and protector to all family members, adult and child, human and canine.

The responsible GSD owner makes sure that her dog is well socialized, approachable and amenable to making new friends.

the rules of acceptable behavior. He still requires training, firm yet gentle and consistent handling by a master who is able to command the dog's respect. Confident breeds like German Shepherds require a strong leader or they will intuitively sense any weakness and assume a dominant role.

Conversely, they are remarkably gentle and tolerant of children if both child and dog are properly trained and socialized together at an early age. Shepherds take their child-care duties seriously!

German Shepherds also have long excelled in all areas of canine competition. In the absence of the opportunity to work, they thrive on sports such as obedience, agility, herding, tracking and Schutzhund, which provide ideal outlets for the breed's instincts and natural proclivity for dog/owner teamwork. Shepherds are also magnificent show dogs and never fail to draw an admiring crowd.

The Shepherd carries a thick double coat that he sheds profusely twice a year and a little bit all year long. Brushing and more brushing is a part of daily life, and Shepherd owners learn to be tolerant of dog hair on furniture and clothing. If you fancy a fur-free household, consider getting a stuffed animal instead.

Unfortunately, the 21st-century German Shepherd is plagued with a multitude of health and temperament problems stemming from his years of ups and downs in popularity. Given his large size, orthopedic problems have long been a curse of the breed, with hip dysplasia first on the list of concerns. Further, as such a popular guard dog, he is often the target of breed-specific legislation in communities that have experienced aggressive behavior in the guardian-dog breeds. If you hope to find a quality

Shepherd, patronize only an experienced and reputable breeder who is honest and forthright, willing to educate you about the pros and cons and available to advise you if problems arise.

Although the German Shepherd has qualities that make him suitable for many a dog lover, a prospective owner must consider the dog's inherent needs before adding one to the household. The ideal Shepherd family must be willing and able to give their dog adequate living space,

plenty of physical and mental exercise, regular grooming and, most importantly, proper training. If you meet those conditions, the German Shepherd will reward you with love and devotion unmatched by any other breed of dog.

No matter where you live, you will be able to find ways to keep your versatile GSD active and invent creative outlets for his considerable talents.

## ARE YOU A GSD PERSON?

### Overview

- A breed like the GSD, which is capable of so much, requires an owner who is just as capable and can devote time, energy and effort into developing his dog's potential.
- The German Shepherd is good for a family that wants to make their dog a true part of their lives. He builds strong bonds of loyalty with those close to him.
- An intelligent dog needs much mental and physical stimulation to prevent boredom and destructive behavior.
- GSDs are wonderful companions for the right people, but prospective owners must first weigh all of the pros and cons.

# Selecting a Breeder

A good German Shepherd puppy is only as good as the breeder who produced the litter. Unfortunately, the Shepherd's popularity after World War I encouraged countless for-profit breeders who were interested only in the bottom line and not in the quality or future of the pups they bred. Health and stability are important in all dog breeds, especially in one as large, powerful and fearless as the Shepherd. Whatever your reasons for wanting a German Shepherd—companionship, dog shows, compe-

Be sure to meet at least one of the parents along with the puppies. All of them should be sound, physically and temperamentally, and be healthy and possess the typical GSD look.

tition or work—you want a healthy dog with a good disposition and correct German Shepherd instincts. Otherwise, why get a German Shepherd? Finding a breeder whom you can trust and who has experience with the breed is paramount and may take time. A good pup (and healthy adult dog) is worth the extra effort.

Looking for a good GSD breeder can be like searching for a needle in a haystack! With such a popular breed, there are many who are in it for the wrong reasons. Consult trusted sources like the AKC and GSD Club of America to direct you to ethical breeders.

Searching for a suitable breeder or puppy can be an emotionally trying experience, taxing your patience and your willpower. All puppies are adorable and it's easy to fall in love with the first cute pup you see, but a poor-quality German Shepherd will have health and temperament problems that can empty your wallet and break your heart. So do your breeder homework before you visit those irresistible furry pups. Arm yourself with a list of questions for the breeder. Then leave your wallet and your kids at home so you aren't tempted to take home a puppy right

It's easy to spot true dedication to the breed by watching the breeder interact with her dogs. Dogs don't lie about love!

away, before you have a chance to carefully decide.

**PEDIGREE AND REGISTRATION PAPERS**

For starters, always ask to see the pedigree and registration papers. Although AKC registration is no guarantee of quality, it is one small step in the right direction. If you hope to show your pup or enter licensed competitions, registration with the AKC is necessary.

The pedigree should include three to five generations of ancestry. Inquire about any titles in the pedigree. Titles such as Ch., CD and SchH I indicate a dog's accomplishments in some area of canine competition, which proves the merits of the ancestors and adds to the breeder's credibility. While it is true that, like the registration, a pedigree cannot guarantee health or good temperament, a well-constructed pedigree is still a good insurance policy and a good starting point.

There should be no extra fee, by the way, for either the pedigree or registration papers. The AKC states that papers do not cost extra, and any breeder who charges for those documents is unscrupulous.

**WHY THIS BREEDING?**

Ask why the breeder planned the litter. A conscientious breeder plans a litter of GSDs for specific reasons and should explain the genetics behind this particular breeding and what he expects it to produce. He never has pups because "his Shepherd is sweet and/or beautiful, his neighbor's dog is handsome, they will have lovely puppies" or "his kids needed to experience the birth of a litter" and so on. Just loving his dog like crazy does not qualify an individual to breed dogs intelligently or properly raise a litter of German Shepherd pups.

Just one look, and who can resist? GSD puppies are undeniably irresistible. Although it will be difficult, don't let "cuteness" be the number-one criterion in your search.

CHAPTER 4

## HEALTH ISSUES AND CLEARANCES

Ask about health issues and clearances. GSDs are prone to hip and elbow dysplasia and osteochondritis dissecans (OCD), three hereditary and potentially crippling joint diseases. Do the sire and dam have hip and elbow clearances from the OFA (Orthopedic Foundation for Animals, a national canine hip registry)? Have the parents' eyes been examined for cataracts and other eye problems within the past year by a board-certified veterinary ophthalmologist? Eye clearances can be registered with the Canine Eye Registry Foundation (CERF). Good breeders will gladly, in fact proudly, provide documentation of all health clearances.

Other health problems recognized in the German Shepherd Dog include epilepsy, hypothyroidism, von Willebrand's disease (vWd), pancreatitis, hemophilia and several skin disorders.

Shepherds are also prone to gastric dilatation/volvulus (bloat), a life-threatening condition that is common in deep-chested breeds such as the German Shepherd, Boxer, Weimaraner, Bloodhound, Great Dane and other similarly constructed breeds. Bloat occurs when the stomach fills rapidly with air and begins to twist, cutting off the blood supply. If not treated immediately, the dog will die. You also can research these and other German Shepherd health problems in more detail on the German Shepherd Dog Club of America's (GSDCA) website (www.gsdca.org) and reputable canine health websites.

## INVOLVEMENT IN THE BREED

Experienced Shepherd breeders are frequently involved in some aspect of the dog fancy with their dog(s), perhaps showing in conformation or training them for

The Orthopedic Foundation for Animals (OFA) was founded by John M. Olin and a group of caring veterinarians and dog breeders in the mid-1960s. The goal of the foundation was to provide x-ray evaluations and guidance to dog breeders with regard to hip dysplasia, a common hereditary disease that affects many different breeds of dog.

Three board-certified OFA radiologists evaluate x-rays of dogs that are 24 months of age or older, scoring their hips as "Excellent," "Good" and "Fair," all of which are eligible for breeding. Dogs that score "Borderline," "Mild," "Moderate" and "Severe" are not eligible for breeding. The sire and dam of your new puppy should have OFA numbers, proving that they are eligible for breeding.

The GSD has a unique sloping topline that can lead to skeletal problems like hip dysplasia when breeders exaggerate this feature.

Since OFA's inception, the organization has expanded to include databases on elbow dysplasia, patellar luxation, autoimmune thyroiditis, congenital heart disease, Legg-Calve-Perthes disease, sebaceous adenitis, congenital deafness, craniomandibular osteopathy, von Willebrand's disease, copper toxicosis, cystinuria, renal dysplasia and other diseases that have hereditary bases in dogs.

Visit the OFA website for more information on the organization, its history, its goals and the diseases from which it safeguards our pure-bred dogs. Go to www.offa.com.

You want a German Shepherd with healthy hips so that he can always be the high-flying athlete that he's meant to be.

some type of performance event or other dog-related activity. Their Shepherd(s) may have earned titles in various areas of competition, which is added proof of the breeder's experience with and commitment to the breed.

Dedicated breeders often belong to the parent club, the German Shepherd Dog Club of America, or an area breed or kennel club. Such affiliation with other experienced breeders and sportsmen expands their knowledge of their chosen breed, which further enhances their credibility. Responsible breeders, by the way, do not raise several different breeds of dog or produce multiple litters of pups throughout the year. One or two litters a year is typical.

## MORE FROM THE BREEDER

Be prepared for the breeder to ask you questions, too…about your history with dogs, previous dogs you have owned, which breeds and what became of these dogs. He will want to know your living arrangements (house, yard, kids, other pets, etc.), your goals for this pup and how you plan to raise him. The breeder's primary concern is the future of his puppies and whether you and your family will be suitable owners who will provide a proper and loving home for his precious little one.

You should be suspicious of any breeder who agrees to sell you a GSD puppy without any type of interrogation. Such indifference indicates a lack of concern about the pups and casts doubt on the breeder's ethics and breeding program.

A good breeder also will warn you about the downside of the German Shepherd. No breed of dog is perfect, nor is every breed suitable for every person's temperament and lifestyle. Be prepared to weigh the bad news with the good about the Shepherd.

## THE SALES CONTRACT

Most reputable breeders have puppy sales contracts that include specific health guarantees and reasonable return policies. Your breeder should agree to accept a puppy back if things do not work out. The breeder also

## AKC LIMITED REGISTRATION

Many breeders place their pet-quality puppies on the AKC's Limited Registration. This does register the pup with the AKC and allows the owner to compete with the dog in some types of AKC-licensed competition, but does not allow AKC

Bring along all family members to meet the breeder, the litter and the other dogs on the premises. Everyone must be in agreement about adding a GSD to the family.

should be willing, indeed anxious, to check up on the puppy's progress after he leaves and be available if you have questions or problems.

registration of any offspring from the mature dog. The purpose of Limited Registration is to prevent indiscriminate breeding of "pet-quality"

German Shepherds. The breeder, and only the breeder, can cancel the Limited Registration if the adult dog develops into breeding quality.

## REFERENCES

If you have any doubts at all, feel free to ask for references…and check them out! It's unlikely that a breeder will offer names of unhappy puppy clients, but calling other owners of the breeder's dogs may make you more comfortable dealing with a particular breeder. A good reference in itself is the breeder's membership with the GSDCA, as member breeders must adhere to a strict Code of Ethics, although you must still ensure that you are comfortable with the breeder.

## WHERE AND WHERE NOT TO LOOK

So how do you find a reputable breeder you can trust? Do your homework before you visit puppies. Check with the AKC and GSDCA for breeder referrals in your area. Their websites also offer links to regional breed clubs and breeders throughout the US. Call and make inquiries. Any information gleaned from these conversations will make you a smarter shopper when you visit a litter of pups.

Ask local veterinarians for referrals. Talk to other GSD owners. Spend the day at a dog show or other dog event where you can meet breeders and exhibitors and get to know their dogs. Most Shepherd devotees are more than happy to discuss the breed, show off their dogs and brag about their accomplishments.

Skip the puppy ads in your local newspaper. Reputable breeders rarely advertise in newspapers. They are very particular about prospective puppy owners and do not rely on mass advertising to attract the right people. Rather, they depend on referrals from other breeders and previous puppy clients. They are more than willing to keep any puppy past the usual eight-week placement age until the right owners come along.

Perhaps the second most important ingredient in your breeder search is patience. You will not likely find the right breeder or litter on your first go-around. Good breeders often have waiting lists, but a good German Shepherd pup is worth the wait.

**SOME FINAL ADVICE**

The end result? You can expect to pay a dear price for all of these breeder qualities, whether you purchase a German Shepherd for a home companion or one for a show or working career. The discount or bargain Shepherd is not a bargain at all. Indeed, the discount pup is in reality a potential disaster that has little chance of developing into a healthy, stable adult. Such "bargains" could ultimately cost you a fortune in vet expenses and heartache that can't be measured in dollars and cents.

## SELECTING A BREEDER

### Overview

- Prospective owners must do their research and choose their breeders carefully. The AKC and GSDCA are trusted sources of breeder referrals; the local paper is not.
- Know what to ask a breeder and what information the breeder should provide.
- Acquaint yourself with the problems to which the GSD can be prone and see proof that the parents are free of these defects.
- Know the traits of a reputable breeder and don't settle for less.
- Choose a breeder with whom you have a good rapport, as he will be an important source of advice throughout your GSD's life.

# Finding the Right Puppy

Are you ready for a new bundle (or basketful) of puppy love to enter your home, family and life?

Your decision to add a German Shepherd to your family is the first small step down the long and exciting road of dog ownership. Finding the right breeder is the next step in your pursuit of the perfect canine companion, and then you must make your actual puppy selection. You may have to travel to visit any litter of pups worth considering. Good Shepherd pups are seldom right around the corner.

A visit to the litter involves much more than puppy hugs and kisses. It's more like your ultimate job interview. While searching for your new German

Shepherd family member, you'll be checking out the applicants…the puppies and their parents, the breeder and the living environment in which the pups are being raised.

Where and how a litter of pups is raised are vitally important to their early development into confident and social animals. The litter should be kept indoors, in the house or in an adjoining sheltered area, not isolated in a basement, garage or outside kennel building. A few very experienced breeders sometimes have separate breeding facilities for their litters, and you will know that you have found one of these exceptional breeders when you see the walls lined with blue ribbons and hundreds of championship certificates.

Whether raised in a breeder's kitchen or kennel, all GSD puppies need to be socialized daily with people and people activities. The greater the pups' exposure to house-

The breeder will ask you all about your lifestyle: type of home, daily routine, other pets, children, etc., to guide you toward the puppy that will grow up to be a perfect fit.

GSD pups are playful and brimming with personality, just like any other pup, but they also have a somewhat serious and quizzical nature befitting the breed's intelligence.

hold sights and sounds between three to four weeks and seven weeks of age, the easier their adjustment to their future human families.

During your visit, scrutinize the puppies as well as their living area for cleanliness as well as signs of sickness or poor health. The pups should be reasonably clean (allowing for normal non-stop "puppy-pies"). They should appear energetic, bright-eyed and alert. Healthy pups have clean, thick coats, are well proportioned and feel solid and muscular without being overly fat and pot-bellied. Watch for crusted eyes or noses and any watery discharge from their noses, eyes or ears. Listen for coughing or mucousy sniffing or snorting. Check for evidence of watery or bloody stools.

Visit with the dam and the sire, if possible. In many cases the sire is not on the premises, but the breeder should at least have photos, his pedigree and a resume of his characteristics and accomplishments. Some Shepherds can be a bit aloof with strangers, but should not shy away from friendly overtures. It is normal for some dams to be somewhat protective of their young, but overly aggressive behavior is unacceptable. Temperament is inherited, and if one or both parents are aggressive or very shy, it is likely that some of the pups will inherit those characteristics.

It's also normal for a new mother to have a rather scrawny coat or be on the thin side after weeks of nursing hungry pups. However, there is a big difference between normal post-partum appearance and signs of poor health or neglect.

Notice how the pups interact with their littermates and their surroundings, especially their response to people. They should be active and outgoing. In most Shepherd litters, some pups will be more outgoing than others, but even a quiet pup that is properly socialized should not be shy or spooky great deal of time cuddling and cleaning up after these pups, and by now know the subtle differences in each pup's personality. The breeder's observations are valuable aids in selecting a

What do you plan to do with your German Shepherd? Look for a pup whose pedigree reflects his ancestors' success in the activities that you wish to pursue.

or shrink from a friendly voice or outstretched hand.

The breeder should be honest in discussing the differences between the puppies' personalities. Although many breeders do some sort of temperament testing, they also have spent a German Shepherd puppy that is right for you and your lifestyle.

Tell the breeder if you plan to show your pup in conformation, compete in other areas or participate in Shepherd-related activities. Some pups will show more

CHAPTER 5

promise for certain pursuits than others, and the breeder can help you select a pup that will best suit your long-term goals.

Do you prefer a male or female? Which one is right for you? Both sexes are loving and loyal, and the differences are due more to individual personalities than to gender. The adult male GSD is, on average, about two inches taller and up to 20 pounds heavier than the female, and thus will appear more powerful and impressive. The female, burdened with heat cycles, can be a bit moody during her hormonal peaks if not spayed. An untrained male can also become

dominant with people and other dogs. A solid foundation in obedience for both genders is necessary if you want your Shepherd pup to respect you as the leader of the pack.

In male puppies, both testicles should be descended into the scrotum. A dog with undescended testicles will make a fine pet but will be ineligible to compete in the show ring. Intact males tend to be more territorial, especially with other male dogs. Altering (neutering or spaying) your male or female Shepherd creates a level playing field and eliminates most of these gender-related differences. Your dog will live longer, too.

By seven weeks of age, the pups should have had at least one worming and their first puppy shots, and have vet's certificates verifying their good health at the time of the exam. Some Shepherd breeders feel that separating

One German Shepherd puppy is cuter than the next, so it's impossible (and unwise) to choose based on looks alone.

the vaccines in a puppy's booster shots reduces the possibility of negative reactions to the various components in the combination vaccines. Ask your breeder and your veterinarian for their recommendations.

The breeder should tell you what the pup has been eating, when and how much. Some send home a small supply of puppy food to mix with your own for the first few days so that, if you are changing the food, it is done gradually. Most breeders also give their clients puppy "take-home" packets that include a copy of the health certificate, the pedigree and registration papers, copies of the parents' clearances and the breeder's sales contract if he has one. Many supply literature on the breed and how to properly raise a German Shepherd pup.

Dedicated breeders know that the more you know, the better life ahead will be for their precious German Shepherd pups. Your goal should be to find a puppy from one of these breeders.

## FINDING THE RIGHT PUPPY

### Overview

- Puppy selection is a decision that requires clear thinking and willpower. Don't just bring home the first puppy that you meet.
- The entire litter should be healthy and sound, kept in a clean area and getting plenty of human contact.
- Meet at least the dam, and possibly the sire, of the litter.
- Take time to observe and interact with the litter, getting to know each pup and the differences between them.
- Consider gender-related differences and your intentions for your pup when making your selection.
- Trust the breeder's advice in guiding you to the best pup for you.

# Welcoming the Puppy

O nce you have found your ideal German Shepherd companion, you can begin the next exciting phase of life with your puppy. For your puppy's safety and your own peace of mind, you need to puppy-proof your house and yard to prevent any accidents that could be dangerous or even fatal for your pup. You also need to shop for your puppy's "wardrobe," those necessities and canine niceties that every puppy requires.

Puppy shopping is the fun part, but hang on to your wallet. Puppy

Your new puppy will be as excited about the big day as you are!

stuff, especially the non-essentials, is often too cute to resist and can easily decimate your budget (and be decimated by puppy teeth!). Start with basic essentials and save the puppy goodies until later.

For a puppy, small bowls made of sturdy, chew-proof materials will be sufficient. As your pup grows, he will need larger bowls, and you may consider elevated bowls if your vet recommends this for better digestive health.

## FOOD AND WATER BOWLS

You'll need two separate serving pieces, one for food and one for water. Stainless steel pans are your best choice, as they are chew-proof and easy to clean. Tip-proof is a good idea, too, since most puppies love to splash about in their water bowls, and the German Shepherd is no exception.

Dietary requirements will change from puppyhood to adulthood, but one thing remains constant: dogs of all ages appreciate treats!

## PUPPY FOOD

Your Shepherd pup should be fed a quality food that is appropriate for his age and breed. Most quality dog foods now offer specific formulas that address the different nutritional needs of small, medium and large (your German Shepherd) breeds of dog during the various stages of their lives. Start with a supply of large-breed growth food, which should be his diet for his first year. After that, you can switch to a large-breed adult-maintenance food.

Your GSD's early growth period as well as his long-term health will benefit from a diet of high-quality puppy and dog food that provides complete nutrition in proper balance, encouraging healthy growth and maintenance. For experienced recommendations, check with your breeder and your vet before you buy your GSD's food.

**COLLARS AND ID TAGS**
Your Shepherd pup should have an adjustable collar that expands to fit him as he grows. Lightweight nylon adjustable collars work best for both pups and adult dogs. Put the collar on your puppy as soon as he comes home so he can get used to wearing it. The ID tag should have your phone number, name and address, but not the puppy's name, as that would enable a stranger to identify and call your dog. Some owners include a line that says "Dog needs medication" to hopefully speed the dog's return if he is lost or stolen. Attach the tag with an "O" ring (the kind used in key rings), as the more common "S" ring snags on carpets and comes off easily.

Today even dog collars have gone high-tech. Some come equipped with beepers and tracking devices. The most advanced pet identification tool uses a Global Positioning System and fits inside a collar or tag. When your dog leaves his programed home perimeter, the device sends a message directly to your phone or email address.

Choke collars and pinch collars are for training

Choose a buckle collar that can be expanded as the puppy grows. Check his collar every day; it can become too tight before you know it.

Three choices of collars, clockwise from upper right: halter, chain choke collar and traditional buckle collar.

purposes and should be worn *only* during training sessions. Training collars should never be used on German Shepherd puppies under 16 weeks of age.

## LEASHES

For your puppy's safety and your own convenience, his leash wardrobe should

When your German Shepherd is accustomed to walking on lead and can do it politely, he can graduate to a flexible lead. This type of lead allows the dog a wider area to explore, but retracts easily when you need to keep him close. Only use a "flexi" designed for large dogs; check the lead's weight limits.

include at least two kinds of leads. A narrow six-foot leather leash is best for walks, puppy kindergarten and other obedience classes, and leash training.

The other lead is a flexible or "flexi" lead. A flexi is an extendable lead housed in a large handle; it extends and retracts with the push of a button. This is the ideal tool for exercising puppies and adult dogs and should be a staple in every GSD's collection. Flexis are available in various lengths (8 feet to 26 feet) and strengths, depending on breed size. Longer is better, as it allows your dog to run about and check out the good sniffing areas farther away from you. They are especially handy for exercising your puppy in unfenced areas or when traveling with your dog.

## BEDDING

Dog beds are just plain fun. Beds run the gamut from

small and inexpensive to elegant, high-end beds suitable for the most royal of dog breeds. However, don't go crazy just yet. Better to save that fancy bed for when your Shepherd is older and less likely to shred it up or make a puddle on it. For puppy bedding, it's best to use a large towel, mat or blanket that can be easily laundered (which will probably be often).

## CRATES AND GATES

These will be your most important purchases for puppy training and safety. A crate is your most valuable tool for housebreaking your pup and his favorite place to feel secure. Crates come in three varieties: wire mesh, fabric mesh and the more familiar plastic airline-type crate. Wire- or fabric-mesh crates offer the best ventilation and some conveniently

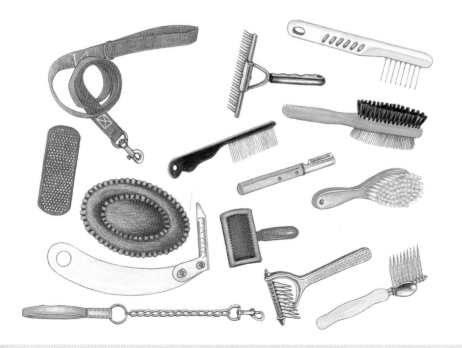

Among the accessories you will need for your puppy are some basic grooming tools. Your need for more equipment will grow right along with your puppy and his dense double coat.

CHAPTER 6

No matter how well your family of canines gets along, each dog must travel in his own crate.

Your active German Shepherd will need plenty of time outdoors to play, exercise and enjoy the fresh air. You must provide him with an escape-proof area, free of hazards like poisonous plants, gardening tools, fertilizers and other chemicals.

will protect your house from the inevitable puppy mischief, and thus save your sanity and keep your puppy safe as well. It's wise to confine the puppy to a tiled or uncarpeted room or space, one that is accessible to the outside door he will use for potty trips. Gated to a safe area where he cannot wreak havoc or destruction, the puppy will soon master Housebreaking 101, chew only appropriate chew toys rather than your antique furniture and spare himself unnecessary corrections for normal puppy mishaps.

fold up suitcase-style. A fabric crate might be a little risky for the youngster who likes to dig and chew.

Whatever your choice, purchase an adult-sized crate, about 24–26 inches wide by about 30 inches high, rather than a small or puppy size; your Shepherd pup will soon grow into the adult-sized crate. Crates are available at most pet stores and through pet-supply catalogs.

A well-placed baby gate

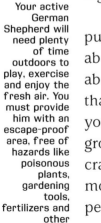

Gated, however, does not mean unsupervised. German Shepherd pups bore easily and have been known to chew through doors and drywall if not given things to occupy them. If your puppy must be unattended, use his crate.

## GROOMING TOOLS

Your basic grooming tool should be a soft bristle brush; any kind will do at this young age. Later, you will need a slicker brush for routine grooming, a steel comb called a Greyhound comb, which has wide- and narrow-spaced teeth, a mat rake and a shedding comb, the latter two being excellent tools for periods of heavy shedding. Be sure to ask your breeder for suggestions on proper grooming aids.

Introduce your puppy to grooming with the soft bristle brush early on so he learns to like the brushing process. It also helps condition the pup

## Puppy Safety at Home

After puppy shopping, you must puppy-proof your house. German Shepherd Dog pups are naturally curious critters that will investigate everything new, then seek-and-destroy just because it's fun. The message here is: never let your puppy roam your house unsupervised. Scout your house for the following hazards:

### Trash Cans and Diaper Pails
These are natural puppy magnets (they know where the good smelly stuff is!)

### Medication Bottles, Cleaning Materials, Roach and Rodent Poisons
Lock these up. You'll be amazed at what a determined puppy can find.

### Electrical Cords
Unplug wherever you can and make the others inaccessible. Injuries from chewed electrical cords are extremely common in young dogs.

### Dental Floss, Yarn, Needles and Thread and Other Stringy Stuff
Puppies snuffling about at ground level will find and ingest the tiniest of objects and will end up in surgery. Most vets can tell you stories about the stuff they've surgically removed from puppies' guts.

### Toilet Bowl Cleaners
If you have them, throw them out now. All dogs are born with "toilet sonar" and quickly discover that the water there is always cold.

### Garage
Beware of antifreeze! It is extremely toxic and even a few drops will kill an adult GSD, less for a pup. Lock it and all other chemicals well out of reach. Fertilizers can also be toxic to dogs.

### Socks and Underwear, Shoes and Slippers, Too
Keep them off the floor and close your closet doors. Puppies love all of the above because they smell like you times 10!

CHAPTER 6

to hands-on attention, which will be invaluable when you have to clean his teeth and ears and clip his nails.

## SOCIALIZATION

This actually puppy-proofs your puppy, not your house. Puppy socialization is your German Shepherd's insurance policy to a happy, stable adulthood and is, without question, the most important element in a Shepherd puppy's introduction to the human world. The German Shepherd is by nature a protective, one-family dog that is very selective of the people he chooses to like and trust. Thus it is most important to expose your pup to strangers and new situations at an early age. Canine research has proven that an unsocialized pup, especially one with protective instincts like the German Shepherd, grows up to be spooky, insecure and fearful of people, children and strange places. Many turn into fear

On the go! You want your puppy's energy to be diverted into safe activities. Proper chew toys are one way to occupy his teeth and mind, and hopefully keep him out of mischief.

biters or become aggressive with other dogs, strangers, even family members. Such dogs can seldom be rehabilitated and often end up abandoned in animal shelters where they are ultimately euthanized. Puppy socialization and early training lay the foundation for a well-behaved adult canine, thus preventing those canine behaviors that lead to the sad situation of abandonment.

The canine's primary socialization period occurs during the puppy's first 20 weeks of life. Once he leaves the safety of his mom and littermates at eight to ten weeks of age, your job begins. Start with a quiet, uncomplicated household for the first day or two, then gradually start to introduce him to the sights and sounds of his new human world. Frequent interaction with children, new people and other dogs is essential at this age. Visit new places (dog-friendly, of course) like parks or community events where there are many people and much activity. Set a goal of two new places per week for the next two months. Keep these new experiences upbeat and happy, which will create a positive attitude in the pup toward future encounters.

"Positive" is especially important when visiting your veterinarian. You don't want a pup that quakes with fear every time he sets a paw inside his doctor's office. Make sure that your vet is a true dog lover as well as a good dog doctor.

Your puppy also will need supervised exposure to children. Puppies of all breeds tend to view little people, like toddlers and small children, as littermates and will attempt to exert the upper paw (a dominance ploy) over the child. Because he was bred to herd and protect, a German Shepherd may become possessive of "his" children and even try to "herd" them. Due to his large size, he could unintentionally overwhelm a small child during play.

A properly bred German Shepherd is generally good with youngsters, but both dog and child must be taught how to behave properly with each other. Teach the children not to tease, run or otherwise entice the puppy into mischievous behavior. Adult family members should supervise and teach the puppy not to nip, jump up or corral the kids.

Take your German Shepherd youngster to puppy school. Some classes accept pups from 10 to 12 weeks of age, with one series of puppy shots as a health requirement. The younger you get started with the pup's education, the easier it is to shape good behavior patterns.

A good puppy class teaches proper canine social etiquette rather than rigid obedience skills. Your puppy will meet and play with young dogs of other breeds, and you will learn about the positive teaching tools you'll need to train your pup. There are many benefits to puppy classes, which provide your pup with essential social-

Along with preparing your home, you and your family will need to be prepared, too. Be ready with lots of love, patience and time for your new friend.

ization and help the two of you lay a solid foundation for his training and good behavior.

Puppy class is important for both novice and experienced puppy folks. If you're a smart Shepherd owner, you won't stop there and will continue on with a basic obedience class. Of course, you want the best-behaved German Shepherd in the neighborhood!

Remember this: there is a direct correlation between the quality and amount of time that you spend with

Your GSD will enjoy the companionship of canine housemates if introductions are made carefully and all are given time to become acquainted on their own terms.

your puppy during his first 20 weeks of life and the character of the adult dog he will become. You cannot recapture this valuable learning period, so make the most of it.

## WELCOMING THE PUPPY

### Overview

- Your home must be prepared for your new puppy in advance of his arrival. This includes having all of the accessories that he requires as well as creating a safe, puppy-proof environment indoors and out.
- Be prepared to invest time in socializing your puppy, as this has much bearing on his adult temperament.
- Introductions between your puppy and children must be done with care and under supervision.
- Consider enrolling in a puppy class, which is beneficial to your efforts in both training and socialization.

# GSD Puppy Kindergarten

**G**erman Shepherds are highly intelligent animals. Their ability to master difficult tasks is testament to their comprehension, trainability and ability, indeed desire, to work as team players. However, that same brilliance can create a challenge for the German Shepherd owner. Your Shepherd will need a solid education in obedience and leadership (yours) if he is to understand and obey the rules of his new human world. Although GSDs are quick learners with a strong desire to please, they also can be possessive

The GSD's protective instincts are beneficial to his owners, when directed in a positive way so that aggression is not encouraged.

and protective of their families and property. Obedience training is the only way to develop a trustworthy canine family member, and this begins on the day that your Shepherd puppy comes home with you.

All dogs are natural pack animals and, as such, they need a leader. Your Shepherd's first boss was his dam, and all of his life lessons came from his mom and littermates. Now you have to assume the role of leader and communicate appropriate behavior in terms that his little canine mind will understand. From a canine perspective, human rules make no sense!

Keep this in mind: the first 20 weeks of any canine's life are his most valuable learning time, a period when his mind is best able to soak up every lesson, both positive and negative. Positive experiences and proper socialization during this period are critical to his future development and stability.

Leaving his comfortable place in the puppy pack and entering the unfamiliar human world is a big step for a young dog.

GSD owners love the companionship of their well-trained dogs. An unruly German Shepherd wouldn't be much fun as a jogging partner!

**CHAPTER 7**

The amount and quality of time you invest with your Shepherd youngster now will determine what kind of an adult he will become.

Canine behavioral science tells us that any behavior that is rewarded will be repeated. That's called positive reinforcement. If something good happens, like a tasty treat or hugs and kisses, a puppy will naturally want to repeat the behavior. That same research

A class picture of a young student and his very first teacher. Now he's graduated and ready for a new instructor— you!

also has proven that one of the best ways to a puppy's mind is through his stomach. Keep your

pockets loaded with puppy treats at all times so you are prepared to reinforce good behavior whenever it occurs.

That same reinforcement principle also applies to negative behavior or what we humans might consider naughty, like digging in the trash can, which the dog or puppy does not know is "wrong." If the pup gets into the garbage, steals food or does anything else that he thinks is fun or makes him feel good, he will do it again. What better reason to keep a sharp eye on your puppy to prevent those normal canine behaviors? He needs to be taught right and wrong through your rewards and corrections.

Rule number one: the puppy must learn that you are now the "alpha" dog and his new pack leader. Rule number two: you have to teach him in a manner he will understand. Remember always that the pup knows nothing about human standards of behavior.

## WORD ASSOCIATION

Use the same word (command) for each behavior every time you teach it, adding food rewards and verbal praise to reinforce the positive. The pup will make a natural connection and will be motivated to repeat the behavior when he hears those key words. For example, when teaching the pup to relieve himself outside, use the same term, like "Go potty," each time he eliminates, adding a "Good boy!" while he's doing his business. Your pup will soon learn what those trips are for.

## IT'S ALL IN THE TIMING

All dogs learn their lessons in the present tense. You have to catch them in the act (good or bad) in order to dispense rewards or discipline. You have three to five seconds to connect with your dog, or he will not understand what he did wrong. Thus, timing and consistency are your keys to success in teaching any new behavior or correcting any bad behavior.

## BASIC PRINCIPLES

Successful puppy training depends on several important principles:

1.  Use simple, one-word commands and say them only once. Otherwise, the puppy learns that "Come" (or "Sit" or "Down") is a three- or four-word command.

2.  Never correct your dog for something he did minutes earlier. Three to five seconds, remember?

3.  Always praise (and treat ) as soon as he does something good (or when he stops doing something naughty).

4.  Be consistent. You can't snuggle together on the couch to watch TV today, then scold him for climbing onto the couch tomorrow.

5.  Never call your dog to come to you and then correct him for something he did wrong. He will think that the correction is for coming to you and will be hesitant to respond to the come

command in the future. (Think like a dog, remember?) Always go to the dog to stop unwanted behavior, but be sure you catch him in the act.

6. Never hit or kick your dog or strike him with an object. Such physical measures will only create fear and confusion in your Shepherd and could provoke aggressive behavior down the road.

7. When praising or correcting, use your best doggie voice. Use a light and happy voice for praise, and a firm, sharp voice for warnings or corrections.

On that note, your dog also will respond accordingly to family arguments. If there's a shouting match, he will think that he did something wrong and head for cover.

## PUPPY GAMES

Puppy games are great ways to entertain your puppy and yourself, while subliminally teaching lessons in the course of having fun. Start with a game plan and a pocketful of tasty dog treats. Keep your games short so you don't push his attention span beyond normal puppy limits.

"Puppy catch-me" helps teach the come command. With two people sitting on the floor about 10 or 15 feet apart, one person holds and pets the pup while the other calls him: "Puppy, puppy, Come!" in a happy voice. When the pup comes running, lavish him with big hugs and give a tasty treat. Repeat back and forth several times…don't overdo it.

You can add a ball or toy and toss it back and forth for the puppy to retrieve. When he picks it up, praise and hug him some more, give him a goodie to release the toy, then toss it back to person number two. Repeat as before.

"Hide-and-seek" is another game that teaches "Come." Play this game outdoors in your yard or another confined safe area. When the pup is distracted, hide behind a tree, bush or other large object. Peek out to see when he realizes that you are gone and comes running back to find you (trust me, he will do that). As soon as he gets close, come out, squat down with arms outstretched and call him: "Puppy, Come!" This is an excellent technique and teaches the puppy to depend on you.

Play "Where's your toy?" by placing one of his favorite toys in plain sight, asking your puppy "Where's your toy?" and letting him take it. Repeat several times. Then place your puppy safely outside the room and place the toy where only part of it shows. Bring him back and ask the same question. Praise highly when he finds it. Repeat several times. Finally, conceal the toy and let your puppy sniff it out.

GSD puppies love to have fun with their people. Games are great teaching aids and one of the best ways to say "I love you" to your puppy.

## GSD PUPPY KINDERGARTEN

### Overview

- The time to start asserting your position as pack leader begins as soon as you bring your puppy home.
- Training is based on basic principles of positive reinforcement for correct behavior or cessation of undesirable behavior. Negative reinforcement is necessary from time to time to correct a pup if caught in a naughty deed.
- Pick simple verbal commands and be consistent.
- Timing is the key to reinforcing good behavior and correcting bad behavior.
- Puppy games are a fun way to spend time with your pup while introducing future commands.

# House-training Your GSD

Your first concern will be teaching your pup to adopt proper toileting habits. Successful house-training is necessary to a peaceable, clean home. Puppy "piles" can be very frustrating for the owner who is not prepared to handle the challenge of teaching the puppy clean habits. Your virtuous patience can and will be tested! Use your dog crate and common sense, and your pup will soon master the basics of potty-training. Structure and schedule are keys to overcoming house-training obstacles. Canines are natural den

Your dog's body language will be evident in telling you that he's about to "go."

creatures, thanks to the thousands of years that their ancestors spent living in caves and cavities in the ground, so puppies adapt quite naturally to crate confinement (a.k.a. structure).

Follow your nose! Like all other dogs, your GSD uses his sense of smell to find a suitable toileting area.

Puppies are inherently clean little fellows and they prefer not to soil their "dens" or living spaces, which makes the crate a natural house-training aid. Thus your pup's crate is actually a multi-purpose dog accessory: his personal dog house within your house, a humane house-training tool, a security measure that will keep puppy safe while protecting your house and belongings when you're not home, a travel aid to house and protect your dog when traveling (most motels will accept a crated dog) and, finally, a comfy dog space for your puppy when your anti-dog relatives come to visit.

A wire crate is preferred for use in the home, as it is very well ventilated and provides your GSD with a clear view, making him feel part of what's going on around him while safely confined.

It's up to you to make sure your GSD's introduction to his crate is a

**CHAPTER 8**

pleasant one. Do so as soon as your puppy comes home so he learns that this is his new "house." For the first day or two, toss a tiny treat into the crate to entice him to go in. Pick a crate command, such as "Kennel," "Inside" or "Crate," and use it every time he enters. You also can feed his first few meals inside the crate with the door still open, so the crate association will be a happy one.

Your puppy should sleep in his crate from his very first night. He may whine or object to the confinement, but be strong and stay the course. If you release him when he cries, you provide his first life lesson: "If I cry, I get out and maybe hugged." Not such a good plan after all!

A better scheme is to place the crate next to your bed at night for the first few weeks. Your presence will comfort him, and you'll also know if he needs a middle-of-the-night potty trip. Whatever you do, do not lend comfort by taking the puppy into bed with you. To a dog, on the bed means equal, which is not a good idea, since you want to establish yourself as the pup's leader.

Make a practice of placing your puppy in his crate for naps at nighttime and whenever you are unable to watch him closely. Not to worry…he will let you know when he wakes up and needs a potty trip. If he falls asleep under the table and wakes up when you're not there, guess what he'll do first? Make a puddle, then toddle over to say "Hi!"

You must become a German Shepherd vigilante. Routines, consistency and an eagle eye lead to house-training success. Puppies always "go" when they wake up (quickly now!), after eating, after play periods and after brief periods of confinement. Most pups under 12 weeks of age will need to eliminate around every hour or so, or about 10 times a day (set your kitchen timer to remind you) .

Always take your puppy outside to the same area, telling him "Outside" as you go out. Pick a "potty" word ("Hurry up," "Go Potty" and "Get Busy" are the most common) and use it when he does his business, lavishing him with "Good puppy, good hurry up" (or what ever your chosen command is) praise. Always use the same exit door for these potty trips, and confine the puppy to the exit area so he can find it when he needs it. Watch for sniffing and circling, sure signs that he needs to relieve himself. Don't allow him to roam the house until he's fully house-trained...how will he find that outside door if he's three or four rooms away? He does not have a house map in his head.

Of course, he will have accidents. All puppies do. If you catch him in the act, clap your hands loudly, say "No!" and scoop him up to go outside. Your voice should startle him and make him stop. Be sure to praise your pup when he finishes his duty outside. It's best to remain positive with your impressionable GSD toddler.

One thing you can count on with your puppy is that accidents can, and will, happen. He doesn't know any better! Be consistent and positive with your house-training routine and the two of you will be living the clean life in no time.

If you discover the piddle spot after the fact...more than three or four seconds later...you are simply too late. Dogs only understand *at the moment* and will not understand a correction given more than five seconds (that's only *five*) after the deed. Correcting any later will only cause fear and confusion. Just forget it and vow to be more vigilant. Never rub your puppy's nose in his mistake or strike your puppy or adult dog with your

CHAPTER 8

hand, a newspaper or other object to correct him. He will not understand and will only become fearful of the person who is hitting him.

House-training hint: remove the puppy's water after 7 p.m. at night to aid in nighttime bladder control. If he gets thirsty, offer him an ice cube. Then just watch him race for the refrigerator when he hears the rattle of the ice-cube tray.

Despite its many benefits, crate use can be abused. Puppies under 12 weeks of age should never be confined for more than 2 hours at a time, unless, of course, they are sleeping. A general rule of thumb is three hours maximum for a three-month-old pup, four or five hours for a four- to five-month-old and no more than six hours for dogs over six months of age. If you're unable to be home to release the dog, arrange for a relative, neighbor or dog-sitter to let him out to exercise and to relieve himself.

One final, but most important, rule of crate use: never, *ever*, use the crate for punishment. Successful crate use depends on your puppy's positive association with his "house." If the crate represents punishment or "bad-dog stuff," he will resist using it as his safe place. Sure, you can crate your pup while you clean up after he has sorted through the trash. Just don't do it in an angry fashion or tell him "Bad dog, crate!" You are crating him to prevent his being underfoot, not as punishment.

If you are adamant about not using a crate (and some people are, for reasons that this author disputes), what, then, do you do with an uncrated puppy when you're not home? (Not a wise choice for a potentially destructive German Shepherd puppy.) Confine him to one area with a dog-proof barrier (like a doggy gate). Puppy-proofing alone may not be enough as, even in a stripped environment, some bored pups will chew through drywall. An exercise pen 4 feet by 4 feet square (available through pet suppliers), sturdy enough that pup can't knock it down, will provide safe containment for short periods. Paper one area for elimination, with perhaps a blanket in the opposite corner for napping. Provide safe chew toys to keep him occupied, but even that is risky at best. If you don't or won't crate your pup and cannot supervise him, be prepared to meet the consequences.

Most importantly, remember that successful house-training revolves around consistency, repetition and word association. Maintain a strict schedule and use your key words consistently. A well-trained owner will have a well-trained German Shepherd, not to mention a clean home and virtually no stress.

## HOUSE-TRAINING YOUR GSD

### Overview

- Teaching the puppy to relieve himself outdoors is the first step to clean living with a well-behaved dog.
- Dogs are natural den creatures that do not like to soil their living quarters, so the crate is a natural house-training aid.
- The puppy should associate his crate only with good things. Learn to use the crate properly.
- Consistency counts! Choose a crate command and a potty command, and establish a toileting routine.
- Remember your timing when rewarding or correcting. "Catch him in the act!"
- Don't ignore the signs! A pup's body language will tell you when he needs to go out.

CHAPTER 9

# Teaching Basic Commands

**A**nti-dog laws are everywhere these days. Most of those laws target the large protection breeds, and many seek to outlaw those breeds from the community. All German Shepherd pups should grow up to be good canine citizens. That's their insurance policy to a welcome mat wherever they may go. They should be proficient in basic commands, such as come, sit, stay, down and heel. Your Shepherd is bright and eager to learn. Start teaching him as soon he comes home. The earlier you start, the more successful you will be!

A well-behaved German Shepherd in public is like an ambassador of good will for the breed, showing that this is an intelligent, even-tempered, polite canine citizen.

Always start your training exercises in a quiet, distraction-free environment. Once your Shepherd pup has mastered a task, change the setting and practice the exercise in another room or the yard. Then practice with another person or a dog nearby. If the pup reacts to the distractions of the new area and does not perform the exercise, back up and continue with the exercise, removing the distractions for a while.

Even the dignified German Shepherd is not above learning fun tricks like "high five."

Appoint one person to instruct your puppy in the early stages so that the pup is not confused. It's the "too-many-cooks" rule of dog training. Once your puppy has learned a command reliably from one person, other family members can join in with the exercise.

Ignore your Shepherd for a few minutes before each training session. The lack of stimulation will make him more eager for your company and attention. Not too long, though—

Use food along with praise in your training program to let your dog know when he's done a good job.

Shepherds don't like to be ignored!

Keep lessons short so your puppy won't get bored or lose his enthusiasm. In time, he will be able to concentrate for longer periods. Vary the exercises to keep his enthusiasm level high and give him breaks for playtime. Watch for signs of boredom and loss of attention.

Always keep your training sessions positive and upbeat. Use lots of praise, praise and more praise! Never train your puppy or adult dog if you are in a grumpy mood. You will lose patience, and he will think it is his fault, which will reverse any progress the two of you have made.

Finish every training session on a positive note. If you have been struggling or unsuccessful with a particular exercise, switch gears and do something he knows well (like the sit) and end the session.

Before you can effectively teach your puppy any command, two things must happen. First, puppy must learn to respond to his name (name recognition) and, second, you must be able to gain and hold his attention. How to accomplish that? Why, with treats, of course! Treats are defined as tiny tidbits, preferably soft easy-to-chew-treats. We don't want to overfeed the pup. Thin slices of hot dogs cut in quarters work well.

## NAME RECOGNITION AND ATTENTION

Start by calling your German Shepherd puppy's name. Once. Not two or three times, but once. Otherwise, he will learn that he has a three-part name and will ignore you when you say it once. Begin by using his name when he is undistracted and when you are sure that he will look at you, and pop him a treat as soon as he does so. Repeat about a dozen times, several times a day. It won't take more than a day or so before he understands that his name means something good to eat if he pays attention.

## A RELEASE COMMAND

Your release command is what you'll use to tell pup that the exercise is over, similar to "At ease" in the military. "All done" and "Free" are most commonly recommended; "Okay" is also used. You'll need this release word to tell your Shepherd that an exercise is finished and it's okay for him to relax and/or move from a stationary position.

## "TAKE IT" AND "LEAVE IT"

These commands offer too many advantages to list. Place a treat in the palm of your hand and tell him "Take it" as he grabs the treat. Repeat three times. On the fourth time, do not say a word when your dog reaches for the treat, just close your fingers around the treat and wait. Do not pull away, but be prepared for the pup to paw, lick, bark and nibble on your fingers. Patience! When he

finally pulls away from your hand and waits for a few seconds, open your hand and tell him "Take it."

Look at this GSD's concentration on his owner as he awaits her command. This is the kind of focus you want from your dog during training sessions.

Now the next step. Show your Shepherd the treat in the palm of your hand and tell him to "Leave it." When he goes for the treat, close your hand and repeat "Leave it." Repeat the process until he finally pulls away on his own, wait just a second, then open your hand and tell him to "Take it," allowing him to take the treat. Repeat the "Leave it" process until he waits just a few seconds, then give the treat on "Take it." Gradually extend the time you wait after your puppy "leaves it" and before you tell him "Take it."

Now you want to teach your German Shepherd to leave things on the ground, not just in your hand. Think of all the things you don't want him to pick up. Position yourself in front of your dog and toss a treat behind you and a little to the side so he can see it, while you say "Leave it." Here begins the dance. If he goes for the treat, use your body and feet, not your hands, to block him, moving him backwards and away from the treat. As soon as he backs off and gives up trying to get around you, unblock the treat and tell him "Take it." Be ready to block again if he goes for it before you give permission. Repeat the process until he understands and waits for the command.

Once your Shepherd knows this well, practice with his food dish, telling him to "Leave it," then "Take it" after he complies (he can either sit or stand while waiting for his dish). As before, gradually extend the waiting period before you tell him to "Take it." This little training exercise sends many messages to your German Shepherd. He is reminded that you're the boss and that all good things, like food, come from his leader who loves him. It will help prevent your puppy from becoming too possessive of his food bowl, a behavior that only escalates and leads to more serious aggressive behaviors. The benefits of a solid take it/leave it are endless.

## COME COMMAND

This command has life-saving potential…preventing your German Shepherd from running into the street, chasing a squirrel or a child on a bike, running away if he inadvertently gets away from you, the list goes on and on.

Always practice the come command on leash and in a safely confined area. You can't afford to risk failure or the pup will learn he does not have to come when called; you want him to respond reliably every time.

Once you have the pup's attention, call him from a short distance: "Puppy, come!" (use your happy voice) and give a treat when he comes to you. If he hesitates, tug him to you gently with his leash. Grasp and hold his collar with one hand as you dispense the treat. The collar grasp is important. You will eventually phase out the treat and switch to hands-on praise only. This maneuver also connects holding his collar with coming and treating, which will assist you in countless future behaviors.

Do 10 or 12 repetitions 2 or 3 times a day. Once your pup has mastered the come exercise, continue to practice daily to imprint this most important behavior onto his brain. Experienced German Shepherd owners know, however, that one can never completely trust a dog to come when called if the dog is bent on a self-appointed mission. Off-leash is often synonymous with out-of-control, so always keep your Shepherd on a leash when not in a fenced or confined area.

## SIT COMMAND

This one's a snap, since your Shepherd already understands the treating process. Stand in front of your pup, move the treat directly over his nose and slowly move it backwards over his head. As he folds backwards to reach the goodie, his rear will move downward to the floor. If the puppy raises up to reach the treat, just lower it a bit. The moment his behind is down, tell him "Sit." That's one word, not three! Release the treat and

A gentle push on the rump will guide your dog into the sit position for the first few times until he understands what is expected of him.

**CHAPTER 9**

gently grasp the collar as you did with "Come." He will again make that positive connection between the treat, the sit position and the collar hold.

As he becomes more proficient, make him hold the sit position longer before you give the treat (this is the beginning of the stay command). Start using your release word to release him from the sit position. Practice using the sit command for everyday activities like sitting for his food bowl or a toy, and do random sits throughout the day, always for a food or praise reward. Once he is reliable, combine the "Sit" and "Leave it" for his food dish. Your German Shepherd is expanding his vocabulary.

**STAY COMMAND**

"Stay" is really just an extension of "Sit," which your Shepherd already knows. With puppy sitting when commanded, place the palm of your hand in front of his nose and tell him "Stay." Count to five. Give him his release word to end the stay and then praise the pup. Increase the stay in tiny increments, making allowances for normal puppy energy.

Once he stays reliably, move your body a step backwards after giving the command, then step forward again. Gradually extend the time and distance that you move away. If puppy moves, say "No" and move back in front of him. Use sensible timelines, depending on your puppy's attention span.

**DOWN COMMAND**

Down can be a tough command to master. Because the down is a submissive posture, some dogs, especially take-charge breeds like the German Shepherd, may find it difficult. That's why it's most important to teach this exercise when your pup is very young.

From the sit position, move the food lure from his nose to the ground and slightly backwards between his front paws. Wiggle it as necessary to spark his interest. As soon as his front legs and rear end hit the floor, give the treat and tell him "Down, good boy, down!" to connect the word to the behavior. This is a tough command to master, so be patient and generous with the praise when he cooperates. Once he goes into the down with ease, incorporate the "Stay" as you did with "Sit." By six months of age, your puppy should be able to do a ten-minute solid sit/stay, ditto for a down/stay.

## WAIT COMMAND

You'll love this one, especially when your Shepherd wants to come in the house with wet or muddy paws. Work on the wait command with a closed interior door. (It would not be wise to try this with an exit to outside.) Start to open the door as if to go through or out. When your dog tries to follow, step in front and body-block him to prevent his passage. Don't use the wait command just yet. Keep

blocking until he hesitates and you can open the door a little to pass through. Then say your wait release word, "Through" or "Okay" or whatever release word you have chosen for this exercise, and allow him go through the door. Repeat by body-blocking until he understands and waits for you, then start applying the command "Wait" to the behavior. Practice in different doorways, using outside entrances (to safe or enclosed areas) only after he will wait reliably.

In the sit/stay, it is helpful to use your palm facing the dog as a stop sign along with your verbal command "Stay."

## HEEL COMMAND

The formal heel command comes a bit later in the learning

curve. A young GSD should be taught to walk politely on a leash, at or near your side. That is best accomplished when your pup is very young and small, instead of 30 or 40 pounds (or more!) pulling you down the street.

Start leash training soon after your pup comes home. Simply attach his leash to his buckle collar and let him drag it around for a little while every day. Play a puppy game while the leash is on. Make wearing his leash a happy moment in

*You don't want a large, strong dog like the German Shepherd pulling you around on the lead. If your GSD tries to lead the way, stand your ground and don't go anywhere until he complies, realizing that you're the one in charge.*

his day. If he chews the leash, distract him with a play activity. You also can spray the leash with a product designed to make it taste unpleasant.

After a few days, gather up the leash in a distraction-free zone of the house or yard and

take just a few steps together. With your puppy on your left side, hold a treat lure at his nose level to encourage him to walk next to you. Pat your knee and use a happy voice. Use the words "Let's go!" as you move forward, holding the treat at his eye level to keep him near. Take a few steps, then give the treat and praise. Move forward just a few steps each time.

Keep these sessions short and happy, a mere 30 to 60 seconds at a time. Never scold or nag him into walking faster or slower; just encourage him with happy talk. Walk straight ahead at first, adding wide turns once he gets the hang of it. Progress to 90-degree turns, using a gentle leash tug on the turns, a happy verbal "Let's go!" and, of course, a treat. Walk in short 10- to 20-second bursts, (that's a long time for a puppy) with a happy break (use your release word) and brief play (nothing wild or crazy, hugs will do nicely) in between. Keep total training time short and always quit with success, even if just a few short steps. Formal heeling will come much later with advanced instruction in a basic obedience class.

## KEEP PRACTICING

All of the basic commands are taught in some phase of a young-dog training class. Check with your vet, breeder or a local kennel club to find one in your area. In addition, there are many books that go into more detail about positive training methods. Consider adding one to your dog library—right next to this one! Helpful information about training and techniques can also be found on the Internet. You and your German Shepherd will both be smarter for your efforts.

Ongoing practice is actually a lifetime dog rule, especially for a strong-willed dog. Dogs will be dogs and, if we don't maintain their skills, they will sink back into sloppy, inattentive behaviors that will be harder to correct. Incorporate the basic commands into your daily routine and your Shepherd will remain a polite canine citizen of whom you can be proud.

## TEACHING BASIC COMMANDS

## Overview

- Make your GSD pup a shining example of all that's good in the breed by ensuring his polite behavior.
- Before beginning your lessons, understand the importance of name recognition, attention and positive reinforcement.
- Basic commands, which include the commands take it/leave it, come, sit, down, stay, heel and wait, are essential not only for good behavior but also for your GSD's safety.
- Practice, practice, practice! Training doesn't end in puppyhood: you will continue on with more advanced exercises as the dog matures, but don't forget to reinforce the basics daily.

**CHAPTER 10**

# Home Care for Your GSD

The average German Shepherd may cope with any of a multitude of health problems that have evolved in the breed since about the mid-20th century. As your dog's primary health care provider, you will have to be proactive with a strong focus on wellness to help keep illness on the back burner of his life. Of course, starting with a healthy puppy bred from genetically healthy parents is the best way to start.

Many common canine diseases can be transmitted from dog to dog. Make sure that your GSD is current on his vaccinations and that you know his canine playmates.

Weight control is an important subject. Veterinarians tell us that over half of the dogs they see are grossly overweight and that such obesity will take two to three years off a dog's life, given the strain it puts on the animal's heart, lungs and joints. The obvious message here: lean is healthier. To determine whether your German Shepherd is at a correct weight, you should be able to feel his ribs beneath a thin layer of muscle with very gentle pressure on his rib cage. When viewing your dog from above, you should be able to see a definite waistline; from the side, he should have an obvious tuck-up in his abdomen.

Keep a record of his weight from each annual vet visit. A few extra pounds? Adjust his food portions (eliminate those table scraps), perhaps switch to a "light," "senior" or lower-calorie dog-food formula and increase his exercise.

A GSD in fit condition should radiate strength, athleticism and musculature.

Swimming is good low-impact exercise, providing the dog with adequate activity without strain on the bones and joints. Be sure that the water is safe and clean before allowing your GSD to take a dip.

Excessive weight is especially hard on older dogs with creaky joints. A senior German Shepherd who is sedentary will grow out of shape more quickly. Walking and running (slower for old guys) are still the best workouts for health maintenance. Tailor your dog's exercise to fit his age and physical condition.

Your weekly grooming sessions should include body checks for lumps (cysts, warts and fatty tumors), hot spots and other skin or coat problems. While harmless skin lumps are common in older dogs, many can be malignant, and your vet should examine any abnormality. Black, mole-like patches or growths on any body part require immediate veterinary inspection. Remember, petting and hugging can also turn up little abnormalities.

Be extra-conscious of dry skin, a flaky coat and thinning hair, all signs of possible thyroid disease. Check for fleas and flea dirt if you think fleas could be present.

Your German Shepherd's vision may deteriorate with age. A bluish haze to the eyes is common in geriatric dogs and does not impair vision, but always check with your vet about any changes in the eyes to determine if these changes represent something harmless or a real problem.

How about your GSD's other end? Does he chew at his rear or scoot and rub it on the carpet? Those are signs of impacted anal glands. Have your vet express those glands (it's not a job for amateurs). Have annual stool cultures done to check for intestinal parasites like hookworms, whipworms and roundworms, which can cause weight and appetite loss, poor coat quality and all manner of intestinal problems, and can weaken your dog's resistance to other canine diseases. See your vet if any of those signs appear. Tapeworms, common parasites that come from fleas, look like grains of rice tucked in the stool.

Heart disease is common in all canines, yet a problem that dog owners frequently overlook. Symptoms include panting and shortness of breath, chronic coughing, especially at night or upon first waking in the morning, and changes in sleeping habits. Heart disease can be treated if it is caught early.

Kidney disease also can be treated successfully with early diagnosis. Dogs seven years of age and older should be tested annually for kidney and liver function. If your dog drinks excessive amounts of water and starts to urinate more frequently, and/or has accidents in the house, run, don't walk, to your vet. Kidney disease can be managed with special diets to reduce the workload on the kidneys.

For everyday common-sense care, every dog owner should know the signs of an emergency. Many dog agencies, humane societies and animal shelters sponsor canine first-aid seminars.

Good health begins with good breeding. Responsible breeders plan each mating with the intentions of eliminating genetic disease and perpetuating only the best characteristics of the breed.

Participants learn how to recognize and deal with signs of common emergency situations, how to assemble a canine first-aid kit, how to give CPR to a dog and more.

Symptoms of problems

**CHAPTER 10**

that require immediate veterinary attention include vomiting for more than 24 hours, bloody or prolonged (over 24 hours) diarrhea, fever (normal canine temperature is 101.5°F) and sudden swelling of the head or any body part (allergic reaction to an insect bite or other stimulus). Also look out for lumps, bumps, bleeding, odor or anything else that seems "off."

Bloat is a real emergency that affects deep-chested breeds like the GSD. Following a meal, the dog's stomach enlarges with gas and then twists on itself, preventing the gas and stomach contents from exiting and also cutting off blood flow. Symptoms include discomfort, anxiety, gagging or dry heaving, exces-

Bee stings, insect bites and visits from other uninvited guests can arise among the flowers. Know how to administer first aid in case these situations arise.

sively salivating, abnormal heart rate and breathing and bloated appearance. Immediate veterinary attention is essential, as shock, followed by death, occurs rapidly.

Other common emergency situations include:

- Heatstroke—Excessive panting, drooling, rapid pulse, dark reddened gums and a frantic, glazed expression (you'll know it when you see it);
- Hypothermia (wet dogs + cold weather)—Shivering, very pale gums, and body temperature under 100°.
- Shock—Severe blood loss from an injury can send a dog into shock. Symptoms include shivering, weak pulse, weakness and listlessness, depression and lowered body temperature.

The lesson here is: know your German Shepherd. Early detection and prompt care are the keys to your dog's longevity and quality of life.

## HOME CARE FOR YOUR GSD

### Overview

- Practice preventative medicine. Keep your GSD well rather than treating illness after it occurs.
- Dog owners must ensure that their dogs stay at a healthy weight. Both obesity and being underweight pose health risks.
- Get in the habit of checking over your dog's skin and coat, making sure he is parasite-free and checking his eyes for good health.
- The earlier that problems are caught and treated, the better the chances for a full recovery.
- Know the symptoms of illness, the signs of emergencies and basic first-aid techniques.

# Feeding Your GSD

The quality of your dog's diet can determine the quality of his health. Top-quality dog foods provide a more digestible product, containing the proper balance of vitamins, minerals and fatty acids necessary for healthy muscle, skin and coat. Canine nutrition research has proven that many cheaper dog foods do not supply the proper nutrients needed to support good health. Research also tells us that, because of the poor nutritional quality in the less expensive foods, you have to feed larger quantities to maintain proper body weight.

No dog will say no to a treat, so don't overdo it! Too many tidbits can upset the balance of your dog's complete diet. Opt for healthy treats and use them wisely.

To keep your German Shepherd in prime condition, feed a quality food that is appropriate for his age and lifestyle. Premium dog-food manufacturers develop their formulas with strict quality controls, using only quality ingredients obtained from reliable sources. The labels on the food containers list ingredients in descending order of weight or amount in the food. Do not add your own supplements, people food or extra vitamins to the dog food. You will only upset the nutritional balance of the food, which could affect the growth or maintenance of your German Shepherd pup or adult. Further, some "people foods" like chocolate, nuts, grapes and onions are actually toxic to dogs.

An important aspect of a dog's diet is plenty of fresh water. Your GSD's water bowl should always be filled with clean water, and be sure to bring some along when away from home.

In the world of quality dog foods, there are enough choices to confuse even experienced dog folks. The major dog-food brands offer foods for every breed size, age and activity

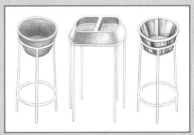

Elevated bowls have long been thought of as a preventative measure against bloat, but debate has ensued over their merit. Discuss bloat-prevention tips and symptoms with your vet and breeder to protect your deep-chested friend from this deadly condition.

level. Puppies require a diet different from that of an adult canine. Growth formulas contain protein and fat levels that are appropriate for puppies of different-size breeds. Large-breed, fast-growing dogs like Shepherds require less protein and fat during the early months of rapid growth, which is better for healthy joint development.

Don't be intimidated by all of those dog foods on the store shelves. Read the labels on the containers to learn what's in these foods and even contact the manufacturer by phone or email. Ask your breeder and your vet for food recommendations. A solid education about dog food will provide the tools to offer your dog a diet that is best for his long-term health. If you plan to switch from the food fed by your breeder, take home a small supply of the breeder's food to mix with your own food to make the change gradual.

## WHEN AND HOW TO FEED?

An eight-week-old puppy does best eating three times a day. (Tiny tummy, tiny meals.) At about 12 weeks of age, you can switch to twice-daily feeding. Breeders suggest two meals a day for the life of the dog, regardless of breed. This is especially important for the deep-chested German Shepherd. Feeding two smaller meals rather than one large one helps digestion and prevents the possibility of bloat, as some theories suggest that gulping large amounts of food or drinking copious amounts of water right after eating can contribute to the condition. Other bloat-prevention measures include no heavy exercise for at least an hour before eating and two hours afterwards. Also make sure that your dog is not overly excited during meals, as it is believed that nervous and overly excited dogs are more prone to this life-threatening condition.

Free-feeding, that is, leaving a bowl of food available all day, is not recommended. Free-feeding fosters picky eating habits...a bite here, a nibble there. Free-feeders are also more likely to become possessive of their food bowls, a problem behavior that signals the beginning of aggression. Scheduled meals give you one more opportunity to remind your German Shepherd that all good things in life come from you, his leader.

With scheduled meals, it's also easier to predict elimination, which is the better road to house-training. In addition, regular meals help you know just how much your puppy eats and when, valuable information for weight control and if your pup gets sick and his appetite changes.

## DRY OR CANNED FOODS?

Should you feed canned food or dry food? Should you offer

### WAYS TO WARD OFF BLOAT

Owners should take precautions to protect their dogs from the possible onset of bloat. Here are some commonsense steps to avoid your dog's swallowing air while he's eating or upsetting his digestion:

• Buy top-quality dog food that is high nutrition/low residue. Test a dry food in a glass of water. If it swells up to four times its original size, try another brand.

• Ask your vet about using bowl stands to elevate your dog's food and water; there is debate over whether this is helpful or harmful.

• No exercise for one hour before and two hours after all meals.

• Never allow your dog to gulp his food or water. Feed him when he is calm, and limit water intake at mealtimes.

• Place large unswallowable objects in his bowl to prevent him from "inhaling" his food in two mouthfuls.

the dry food with or without water? Dry food is recommended by most vets, since the dry particles help clean the dog's teeth of plaque and tartar. Adding water to dry food is optional. The "food hog" who almost inhales his food will do better with a splash of water in his food pan to slow his food intake. A bit of water added immediately before eating is also thought to enhance the flavor of the food while still preserving the dental benefits. Your GSD needs plenty of water, but it is thought that limiting water at mealtimes is best for bloat prevention.

## HOW MUCH FOOD?

Like people, puppies and adult dogs have different appetites; some will lick their food bowls clean while others just pick at their food. It's easy to overfeed a chow hound. Who can resist those soulful Shepherd eyes? Be strong! Chubby puppies may be cute and cuddly, but the extra weight will stress their growing joints and is thought to be a factor in the development of hip and elbow disease. Overweight pups also tend to grow into overweight adults

who tire more easily and will be more susceptible to other health problems. Consult your breeder and your vet for instructions on how to best increase meal portions as your puppy grows.

## LEAN IS IN

Always remember that lean is healthy, fat is not. Research has proven that obesity is a major canine killer. Quite simply, a lean dog lives longer than one who is overweight. And that doesn't even reflect the better quality of life for the lean dog that can run, jump and play without the burden of an extra 10 or 20 pounds.

If your adult dog is overweight, you can switch to a "light" food which has fewer calories and more fiber. To check your dog's figure, you should be able to see a "waistline" when viewing your dog from above, and see a "tuck-up" in the abdominal area when viewing from the side. "Senior" foods for older dogs have formulas designed to meet the needs of less active, older dogs. "Performance" diets contain more fat and protein for dogs that compete in sporting disciplines or lead active lives.

## TRY IT RAW!

To complicate the dog-food dilemma, there are also raw foods available for those who prefer to feed their dogs a completely natural diet rather than traditional manufactured dog food. The debate on raw and/or all-natural vs. manufactured dog food is a fierce one, with some proponents claiming that raw diets have cured their dog's allergies and other chronic ailments. If you are interested in this alternative feeding method, be sure to educate yourself on canine nutrition. Check with your vet, ask your breeder and read up on the subject.

## THE BEST DIET

The bottom line is this: what and how much you feed your dog is a major factor in his overall health and longevity. It's worth your investment in extra time and dollars to provide the best diet for your dog.

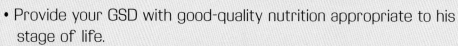

**FEEDING YOUR GSD**

**Overview**

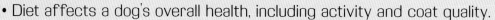

- Provide your GSD with good-quality nutrition appropriate to his stage of life.
- Diet affects a dog's overall health, including activity and coat quality.
- Ask your breeder and vet for advice about the GSD pup's food, feeding schedules, amounts and how to make changes.
- Although the deep-chested GSD is prone to bloat, there are simple daily preventatives that you can incorporate to protect your dog.
- Maintain your GSD in fit condition with a proper feeding and exercise regimen.

**CHAPTER 12**

# Grooming Your GSD

A handsome German Shepherd is a well-groomed German Shepherd, and vice versa. However, a clean, healthy-looking coat is just one facet of your dog's grooming program. Total grooming also involves your Shepherd's skin, teeth, ears, nails and feet, as well as safety checks for lumps, bumps and other abnormalities that can hide beneath your dog's dense coat. Such hands-on care will uncover any tiny critters, like fleas or ticks, which may be stowing away on your dog. Let's not forget the

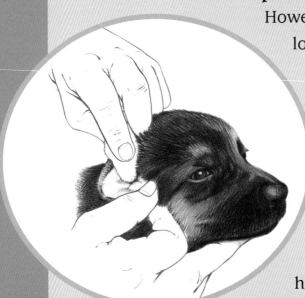

Use a cotton ball or other soft wipe to gently clean your pup's outer ear. Never probe into the ear canal.

bonding benefits of one-on-one personal attention. Good grooming habits, established early in your German Shepherd's life, should be a daily to weekly process all year long.

Ideally, your Shepherd should enjoy being groomed; after all, it's the next best thing to petting. To that end, introduce the brush, nail clippers and toothbrush when he is just a pup. Dogs who have not experienced these ministrations early in life may object when they are older…and bigger…and better able to resist. Grooming will then become a distasteful chore, even a battle, rather than a routine procedure that both of you can enjoy. The moral here: start young.

A grooming rake is good for use on double-coated dogs, as it gets down to the undercoat to remove any dead hair.

## BRUSHING

Hold your first grooming session as soon as your Shepherd puppy has adjusted to his new home base. Start with tiny increments of time, stroking

Use grooming time to check your GSD's dense coat all the way down to the skin, looking for signs of parasites, debris picked up from outdoors or any other irritants.

him gently with a soft brush, briefly handling his paws, looking inside his ears, gently touching his gums. Use lots of encouraging sweet talk and offer little bits of dog treats during each session. Ah, the power of positive association!

The adult German Shepherd has a medium-length double coat, with an undercoat that varies in density depending on the climate in which he is raised. Vigorous weekly brushing will remove dust and distribute the oils that keep his coat clean and conditioned, with more frequent (daily!) brushing needed during shedding season. Brush first opposite the grain to remove dead hair and debris, then brush with the grain to smooth the fur.

**BATHING**
Frequent bathing is seldom necessary and, in fact, will remove the essential oils that keep your dog's skin supple and his coat soft and gleaming.

Frequent brushing is the best way to clean the coat and keep it in super sheen.

How often should you bathe your German Shepherd? In most cases, no more than every few months and less often if your dog stays out of mud holes and does not roll around in smelly stuff. A warm bath during your Shepherd's semi-annual shedding period will help strip out all that loose undercoat. Otherwise, frequent bathing is seldom necessary.

Bathing rituals can be a challenge if your dog dislikes water or getting lathered up. To minimize the stress and struggle of bath time, start when your pup is small. Imagine wrestling over 70 pounds of adult GSD into the tub or shower stall!

Lure your puppy into the tub with the usual food rewards. Line the tub or shower stall with a towel for safe footing. Start with a dry tub. After the pup is comfortable there, gradually add shallow water and the bathing process. He may never learn to love it, but all you need is his cooperation.

After shampooing, always rinse the coat completely to avoid any itching from residual shampoo. A good chamois is the ideal tool for drying, as it absorbs water like a sponge. Keep him away from drafts for a good while after bathing and drying to prevent him from becoming chilled. Spritz-on dry shampoos are handy in case you need a quick clean-up to remove dirt or body odor.

### DENTAL HYGIENE

Dental hygiene is as important for canines as it is for humans. Plaque and tartar build-up can lead to gum disease, which is a harbinger of more serious diseases. Clean teeth are good preventative medicine and something over which you have complete control.

A daily toothbrushing is the ideal, but twice weekly may be more realistic. Start cleaning his teeth while your Shepherd is a pup and use positive associations like petting and praise during brushing. Begin by just rubbing your finger around his gums and over his puppy teeth. Graduate to a doggie toothbrush or simply use a gauze pad wrapped around your index finger. Toothpaste formulated for dogs

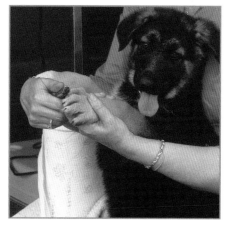

No dog enjoys getting pedicures, but at least you want your GSD to cooperate. Accustom your GSD to nail clipping as a pup so it's second nature and no problem for him as an adult.

will enhance the process; "people" paste will make him sick. Your Shepherd will also learn to accept your hand in his mouth, which is a big plus for bite prevention.

Studies by the American Veterinary Dental Association

show that 80% of dogs exhibit signs of oral disease as early as age three. Further studies prove that good oral hygiene can add three to five years to a dog's life. Need we say more?

**NAIL TRIMMING**

Nails should be trimmed at least once a month. This is always the least favorite grooming chore, and the one most often neglected. Early introduction will help make the process easier. Puppies do not naturally like pedicures, so start nail clipping as soon as possible, since the longer you wait, the less he will cooperate. Try to make it a positive experience so that he at least tolerates it without a major battle. Offer those puppy treats with each clipping session so your puppy will learn that when you touch his paws or trim those nails, he will receive a food reward.

At first you may have to settle on only one or two nails at a time to avoid a wrestling match. That's a good start. It is better to trim a small amount of nail more frequently than trying to cut back a nail that has grown too long. Nip off the nail tip or clip at the curved part of the nail. Be careful not to cut the quick (the pink vein in the nail), as that is quite painful and may cause the nail to bleed profusely. If you accidentally snip a quick, you can stanch the bleeding with a few drops of a clotting solution available from your veterinarian. Keep it on hand…accidents happen.

**EAR CARE**

Weekly ear checks are worth the proverbial pound of cure. Ear infections are common to all breeds of dog, with some breeds more prone to chronic ear infection than others. The German Shepherd's upright ears are not as prone to the ear infections and hematomas that often plague the flop-eared breeds. However, weekly ear checks are still a necessity, since ear infections are easier to treat if caught early.

Use a cotton ball or pad to clean the folds of the upper ear, but never probe inside so that you avoid puncturing the ear drum. Regular cleansing with a specially formulated ear cleanser obtained through your veterinarian will keep your dog's ears clean and odor-free.

Symptoms of ear infection include redness and/or swelling of the ear flap or inner ear, a nasty odor or a dark, waxy discharge. If your Shepherd digs at his ear(s) with his paw, shakes his head a lot or appears to lose his balance, see your vet at once.

The two most common mistakes owners make when dealing with ear infections are waiting too long to seek treatment and failing to treat the ear for the entire course of medication, which allows the infection to smolder and sprout up again. Be proactive with your Shepherd's ear care and the better he'll hear you say, "Get outta the trash!"

## GROOMING YOUR GSD

### Overview

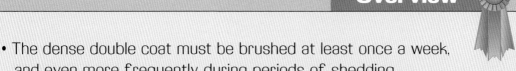

- The dense double coat must be brushed at least once a week, and even more frequently during periods of shedding.
- Frequent bathing is neither necessary nor beneficial.
- Accustom your GSD to his toothbrush and nail clippers early in life.
- Ear care means keeping the ears clean and making sure they are free of infection and infestation.
- Consider your total grooming routine as an extension of home health-care. He will be more handsome, too!

# Keeping the GSD Active

The German Shepherd is a highly intelligent dog who needs to be active and mentally stimulated to maintain his physical and emotional health. A well-exercised Shepherd is happily tired and less inclined to find mischievous outlets for his unexpended energy. A Shepherd owner will benefit as well, since daily exercise is good for humans too!

Neither the German Shepherd

Up and over the A-frame with ease, the German Shepherd makes short work of most obstacles once he's learned how to navigate them.

puppy nor adult will get proper exercise on his own. His incentive is you, the person in charge! Long, brisk walks twice a day will help keep your Shepherd fit and trim, as well as keep his brain stimulated through experiencing the sights and sounds of the neighborhood.

How long and how far to walk will depend on your Shepherd's age, physical condition and energy level. A young Shepherd's bones are softer and more vulnerable to injury during his first 12 to 15 months of life and should not be subjected to heavy stress. That means shorter walks and no games or activities that encourage high jumping or heavy impact on his front or rear until he is past the danger age. Playtime with other canines also should be supervised to avoid excessive wrestling and twisting. Swimming, whenever possible, is excellent low-impact exercise.

Conformation showing is popular with dogs and fanciers of all breeds, and the German Shepherd is something to see as he confidently moves around the ring.

Sleeve training, shown here, is a component of Schutzhund work, which should only be undertaken with the help of an experienced, knowledgeable trainer.

On warm days, avoid walking during midday heat and go out during the cooler morning or evening hours. If you're a jogger, your adult Shepherd buddy is the perfect running partner if he is in good physical condition. Jogging on turf or other soft surfaces is easier on your Shepherd's joints and feet. Just make sure that your dog is healthy and fully developed before he joins you.

Daily walks are also excellent bonding sessions. Your GSD will consider his walks more than merely exercise and will look forward eagerly to his special time with you.

You can also plan a weekly night out together and enroll in a training class. The benefits of obedience class are endless. You will be motivated to work with your dog daily so you don't look unprepared at each week's class. You'll both be more active. Your dog will learn the basics of obedience and will become a model citizen. He will discover that you really are the boss!

Agility classes offer even more healthy outlets for a German Shepherd's energy. Your dog will learn to navigate all sorts of jumps and obstacles. The challenge of learning to navigate these agility obstacles, and his success in mastering each one, will make you proud of both of you! Be sure to work on surfaces of a resilient material to limit impact on your dog's bones and muscles. Do not begin working with your GSD in agility until he has reached 12 months of age.

You can also compete with your dog in obedience and agility trials. German Shepherds excel at both and often place among the top-scoring dogs.

Schutzhund work offers yet one more opportunity for the GSD to demonstrate his natural skills and ability. *Schutzhund* is a German word, meaning "protection dog." A Schutzhund-trained dog is trained to ward off dangerous situations, as opposed to acting as an attack dog. Training, done with the help of a professional, includes three levels of difficulty in three areas: tracking, obedience and protection.

Schutzhund trials are most popular in Germany, where they originated. In the US, trials are held under international rules. The United Schutzhund Club of America is the largest Schutzhund organization in the US, with over 155 member clubs.

Conformation showing is by far the most popular canine competition activity for all breeds. If you plan to show your German Shepherd, make sure you look for a show-quality puppy and discuss your goals with the breeder. Many local breed clubs host conformation training classes and can help a novice get started.

To get started in any area of the dog sport, find a club or join a training group. Working with other fanciers will give you the incentive to keep working with your dog. Check the GSD clubs' and the AKC's websites for details and contact people.

## KEEPING THE GSD ACTIVE

## Overview

- The intelligent, athletic German Shepherd needs constructive ways to expend his considerable energy.
- Take it easy with the puppy's exercise, as he's more prone to bone, joint and muscle injury during his crucial growth stage.
- The adult GSD has the stamina to join you on long walks and jogs.
- Take your activities to the next level and train your GSD for obedience, agility or another area of the dog sport.
- Clubs and classes help you to get started in the activity of your choice while providing the opportunity to meet other fanciers who share your interests.

CHAPTER 14

# Your GSD and His Vet

An experienced, trustworthy vet is as important as a good breeder. Ask your dog-owning friends for recommendations and check with the local kennel or breed club. Your Shepherd's long-term health depends on quality long-term veterinary care.

Take your puppy for a veterinary exam within the first few days of bringing him home. Show the vet the records of shots and wormings from your breeder. The vet will conduct a thorough exam to make sure your pup is in good health,

Your vet will manage all aspects of your pup's vaccinations. Discuss the safest method of inoculating your pup and keep his scheduled appointments for shots.

and will schedule vaccinations, microchipping, routine medications and regular well-puppy visits. A good vet will be gentle and affectionate with a new pup and do everything possible to make sure that the puppy is not frightened.

Vaccine protocol for puppies varies with many veterinarians, but most recommend a series of three "combination" shots given at three- to four-week intervals. Your puppy should have had his first shot before he left his breeder. Many breeders and veterinarians feel the potency in high-combination vaccines can negatively compromise a puppy's immature immune system, so they recommend fewer vaccines in one shot or even separating vaccines into individual injections.

The wisest and most conservative course is to administer only one shot in a single visit. That means extra trips to your vet, but your German

Be aware of small bumps, lumps and any abnormalities that may turn up when petting your dog. Problems can arise that aren't obvious to the eye, and veterinary attention should be sought at first notice.

You want your German Shepherd Dog to share many happy, healthy, active years as a member of your family.

Shepherd's healthy immune system is worth it!

## VACCINES AND REGULAR VISITS

The vaccines recommended by the American Veterinary Medical Association include: distemper, fatal in puppies; canine parvovirus, highly contagious and also fatal in puppies and at-risk dogs; canine adenovirus, highly contagious and high risk for pups under 16 weeks of age; and canine hepatitis, highly contagious, pups at high risk. Rabies vaccination is mandatory in all 50 states.

Vaccines no longer routinely recommended by the AVMA, except when the risk is present, are canine parainfluenza, leptospirosis, canine coronavirus, bordetella (canine cough) and Lyme (borreliosis). Your veterinarian will alert you if your pup needs these shots.

Research suggests that annual vaccinations may actually be over-vaccinating. Mindful of that, the revised AVMA brochure on vaccinations suggests that veterinarians and owners consider dogs' individual needs before they vaccinate. Many dog owners now have titer tests done to check their dogs' antibodies rather than automatically vaccinating for parvo or distemper.

Regardless of vaccine frequency, every German Shepherd should visit his veterinarian once a year. At the very least, he needs an annual heartworm test before he can receive another year of medication. Most importantly, the annual visit keeps your vet apprised of your pet's health progress, and the hands-on exams often turn up small abnormalities. Always ask your vet what shots or medications your dog is getting and what they are for. A well-informed dog owner is better prepared to raise a healthy dog.

## COMMON PARASITES

Heartworm is a parasite that propagates inside your dog's heart and will ultimately kill your dog. Now found in all 50 states, heartworm is delivered through a mosquito bite. Even indoor dogs should take a heartworm preventative, which can be given daily or monthly in pill form, or in a shot given every six months. Heartworm preventatives are prescription medications, and a heartworm test is required before the vet will dispense the medication.

Fleas have been around for centuries, and it's likely that you will wage flea battle sometime during your German Shepherd's lifetime. Fortunately, today there are several low-toxic effective flea weapons to aid you in your war against these pests.

Three tick-borne diseases, Lyme disease, ehrlichiosis and Rocky Mountain spotted fever, are now found in almost every state and can affect humans as well as dogs. Dogs that live in or visit areas where ticks are present, whether seasonally or year-round, must be protected.

## KNOW YOUR DOG!

Your German Shepherd's health is in your hands between his annual visits to the vet. Be ever-conscious of any changes in his appearance or behavior. Things to consider:

Has your German Shepherd gained a few too many pounds or suddenly lost weight? Are his teeth clean and white? Is he urinating more frequently or drinking more water than usual? Does he strain during a bowel movement? Any changes in his appetite? Does he appear short of breath, lethargic, overly tired? Have you noticed limping or any sign of joint stiffness? Is he exhibiting symptoms that could indicate bloat?

These are all signs of serious health problems that you should discuss with your vet as soon as they appear. This is very important for the senior dog, since even minor changes can be indicative of something serious. In the case of bloat symptoms, veterinary attention is required right away, as shock and death can ensue very quickly in dogs of any age.

## SPAYING/NEUTERING

Spay/neuter is the best health insurance policy you can give your German Shepherd. Statistics prove that females spayed before their first heat cycle (estrus) have 90% less risk of several common female cancers and other serious female health problems. Males neutered before their male hormones kick in, usually before six months of age, enjoy zero to greatly reduced risk of testicular and prostate cancer and other related tumors and infections. Additionally, males will be less likely to roam, become aggressive or display those overt male behaviors that drive most people nuts.

Statistically, by having your GSD spayed or neutered, you will be helping to reduce the pet overpopulation problem and adding to your dog's long-term health.

## YOUR GSD AND HIS VET

### Overview

- Finding a good vet is one of the most important things you can do for your GSD.
- Your vet will manage all aspects of your GSD's vaccination program. Discuss the safest way in which to inoculate your dog.
- Your adult GSD needs a thorough veterinary exam annually.
- Protecting your GSD against internal and external parasites is essential.
- Recognize changes in your GSD so that you can contact the vet at the first indication of anything abnormal.
- Spaying/neutering offers many health benefits, including protection from cancers and other diseases of the reproductive organs.

# Look in the garden

**Story by Jenny Giles**     **Illustrations by Margaret Power**

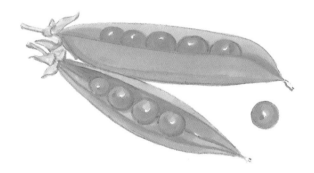

After school,

Scott went home with James.

"I'm hungry," said James.

"Let's eat some peas."

"Peas?" said Scott.

3

"I don't like peas," said Scott.

"I like cookies."

"You will like my peas,"
said James. "Come with me."

Scott went with James,
but he was not very happy.

The boys went into the garden.

Scott looked around.

"Where are the peas?" he said.

"They are over here," said James.

"But peas don't look like that!"
said Scott.

7

"They look like that in a garden,"
said James.
"This is a pod,
and the peas are inside it."

James opened one of the pods.

Scott looked at the little green peas.

9

"Here, have some!" said James.

Scott had some of the peas.
Then he smiled.
"I **like** the peas
from your garden," he said.

The boys opened some of the pods.

They stayed in the garden, eating peas.

Then Scott's mom came.

"Where are you, Scott?" she said.

"It's time to go home!"

"I'm over here, eating peas!" said Scott.

13

"But you don't like peas,"
said his mom.
"You won't eat peas at home!"

Scott smiled.
"I will now," he said.
"Can I have a garden
and plant some peas, like James?"

"I like peas out of the pod!"
said Scott.